Yellowstone National Park

by Audra Wallace

Content Consultant

Nanci R. Vargus, Ed.D.
Professor Emeritus, University of Indianapolis

Reading Consultant

Jeanne M. Clidas, Ph.D.
Reading Specialist

Children's Press®
An Imprint of Scholastic Inc.

Library of Congress Cataloging-in-Publication Data
Names: Wallace, Audra, author.
Title: Yellowstone National Park/by Audra Wallace.
Description: New York, NY: Children's Press, an imprint of Scholastic Inc., 2018. | Series: Rookie national parks | Includes bibliographical references and index.
Identifiers: LCCN 2016051665| ISBN 9780531233351 (library binding: alkaline paper) | ISBN 9780531239070 (paperback: alkaline paper)
Subjects: LCSH: Yellowstone National Park—Juvenile literature.
Classification: LCC F722 .W335 2018 | DDC 978.7/52—dc23
LC record available at https://lccn.loc.gov/2016051665

Produced by Spooky Cheetah Press
Design: Judith Christ-Lafond/Brenda Jackson/Joan Michael

Published in 2018 by Children's Press, an imprint of Scholastic Inc., 557 Broadway, New York, NY 10012.

Printed in China 62

SCHOLASTIC, CHILDREN'S PRESS, ROOKIE NATIONAL PARKS™, and associated logos are trademarks and/or registered trademarks of Scholastic Inc.

1 2 3 4 5 6 7 8 9 10 R 27 26 25 24 23 22 21 20 19 18

Table of Contents

Introduction **5**

1. Steaming Springs **9**

2. Gushing Geysers **13**

3. Mega Mud Puddles **16**

4. That's Wild! **21**

Field Guide **26**

Where Is Ranger Red Fox? **28**

Leaf Tracker **30**

Glossary **31**

Index **32**

Facts for Now **32**

About the Author **32**

Yellowstone has lakes, forests, and mountains.

I am Ranger Red Fox, your tour guide. Are you ready for an amazing adventure in Yellowstone?

Welcome to Yellowstone National Park!

Yellowstone (**yel**-oh-stone) was America's first-ever **national park**. People visit national parks to explore nature.

Yellowstone was established in 1872. It is mostly in Wyoming. Parts of it are also in Idaho and Montana.

Millions of years ago, volcanoes helped form Yellowstone. The volcanoes **erupted** and lava flowed out.
As the lava cooled, it hardened into rocks. This happened over and over. The rocks became Yellowstone's mountains and canyons.

Mount Washburn is a volcano in Yellowstone.

United States

←Wyoming

Yellowstone
National Park

N
W E
S

Mount Washburn last erupted hundreds of thousands of years ago.

Grand Prismatic Spring is the largest hot spring in Yellowstone. It is bigger than a football field!

There are thousands of hot springs in Yellowstone.

Chapter 1

Steaming Springs

Red-hot **magma** from Yellowstone's volcanoes still boils right below the park's surface. It creates the hot springs, geysers (**gye**-zurs), and mud pots that make the park famous.

Hot springs are boiling pools of water. They form when water from rain and snow seeps underground. Magma heats the water. The hot water bubbles back to the surface. It rises through holes in the ground.

Water flows down step-like rocks called terraces.

The colors of the water come from tiny creatures living in it.

The Mammoth Hot Springs area has many pools of water. There are a lot of **minerals** in the water. When the water cools, the minerals are left behind. The minerals harden. They build up near the pools. They form layers that look like steps.

Steamboat Geyser shoots up to 300 feet (91 meters) in the air. That is as high as a stack of 30 school buses!

Look out! Geysers shoot steam and hot water.

Chapter 2

Gushing Geysers

A geyser is a type of hot spring. But with a geyser, at times the water bursts into the sky like a fountain!

There are about 500 geysers in Yellowstone. That is more than any other place on Earth. Steamboat Geyser is the tallest geyser in the park. It is also the tallest in the world.

Some people try to guess when Old Faithful will erupt next.

Old Faithful is another famous geyser. It erupts about every 60 to 100 minutes. That is how it got its name. The word *faithful* describes someone or something you can depend on.

This photo of Old Faithful was taken in 1872.

In the late 1800s, soldiers washed their dirty clothes in Old Faithful!

Chapter 3

Mega Mud Puddles

If you ever visit Yellowstone, you may see people holding their noses. Why? Some parts of the park smell like rotten eggs! The smell comes from pools of water called mud pots. Mud pots are brown and goopy and very hot. The water inside them is mixed with clay.

The mud in some pots is hotter than 150°F (66°C).

Gases make the mud pots bubble.

Do not even think about making mud pies with this stuff!

The mud pots have fun names like Mud Volcano and Artists' Paintpots. But watch out! Mud pots can explode. Some shoot hot mud up to 15 feet (4.6 meters) in the air.

One mud pot called Black Dragon's Cauldron burst in 1948. It knocked down trees and covered a forest in thick mud. What a mess!

Mud pots are, well, muddy because they do not contain a lot of water.

Colorful mud gives Artists' Paintpots their name.

19

Bison graze in
Yellowstone's valleys.

Bison are
sometimes called
buffalo. But bison
and buffalo are
different animals.

Chapter 4

That's Wild!

Yellowstone is home to many animals and plants. Bison, grizzlies, and gray wolves are its most famous animals. All of them were once in danger of dying out. But they have all made big comebacks in the park.

Bison are the easiest to spot. They are the biggest land animals in North America!

Grizzly bears were once found across the United States. Today, Yellowstone is one of the few places where wild grizzlies live.

About 100 gray wolves prowl the park. A long time ago, people killed all of the gray wolves in Yellowstone. In 1995, they were brought back to the park.

I'm not hanging around if wolves are nearby!

Both grizzlies and gray wolves hunt elk.

Grizzlies search for berries to gobble up.

Most of the trees in Yellowstone are conifers (**kah**-nuh-furs), or evergreens. In spring, wildflowers fill the landscape with a rainbow of colors.

About four million people go to the park each year. They gaze at wildflowers and waterfalls. They hike to mountains and mud pots. They raft down the Yellowstone River. No wonder Yellowstone is such a hot spot to visit!

There is so much to see and do in Yellowstone!

Imagine you could visit Yellowstone. What would you do there?

These are just some of the incredible animals that make their home in Yellowstone.

bison

gray wolf

prairie dog

bald eagle

mountain lion

badger

Wildlife by the Numbers
The park is home to about...

285 species of birds

67 species of mammals

The Yellowstone cutthroat trout is found nowhere else on Earth.

grizzly bear

Yellowstone cutthroat trout

elk

red fox

trumpeter swan

11 species of reptiles and amphibians

16 species of fish

Where Is Ranger Red Fox?

Oh no! Ranger Red Fox has lost his way in the park. But you can help. Use the map and the clues below to find him.

1. Ranger Red Fox fell asleep near Mammoth Hot Springs.

2. He woke up and walked south. He saw a geyser that gushed water about every hour.

3. Next, he headed northeast to see the Mud Volcano.

4. Finally, he hiked west. He ended up by a huge, rainbow-colored pool.

Help! Can you find me?

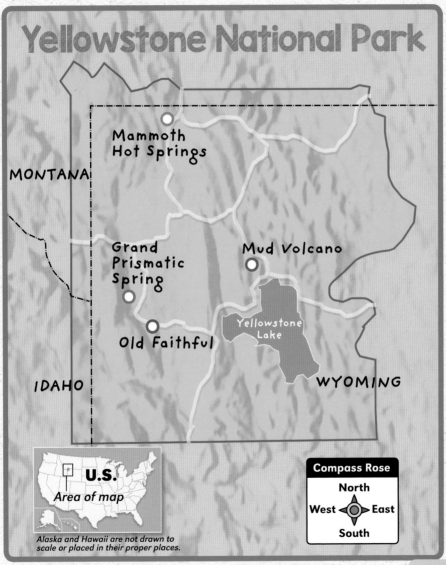

Yellowstone National Park

MONTANA

Mammoth
Hot Springs

Grand
Prismatic
Spring

Mud Volcano

Yellowstone
Lake

Old Faithful

IDAHO

WYOMING

U.S.
Area of map

Alaska and Hawaii are not drawn to
scale or placed in their proper places.

Compass Rose

North
West ◆ East
South

Leaf Tracker

Can you guess which leaf belongs to which tree in Yellowstone? Read the clues to help you.

1. Lodgepole pine
Clue: This tree's leaves are dark green. They are long and thin.

2. Quaking aspen
Clue: This tree has rounded, triangle-shaped leaves. They turn yellow in fall.

3. Rocky Mountain juniper
Clue: The leaves of this tree are blue-green. Small gray berries hang from the branches.

Answers: 1. C; 2. B; 3. A

Glossary

erupted (i-**ruhpt**-ed): suddenly and violently threw out lava, hot ashes, and steam

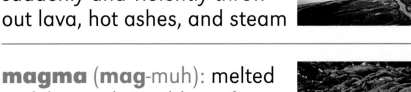

magma (**mag**-muh): melted rock beneath Earth's surface; becomes lava when it flows out of volcanoes

minerals (**min**-ur-uhls): solid substances that make up rock, sand, and soil

national park (**nash**-uh-nuhl pahrk): area where the land and its animals are protected by the U.S. government

Index

Artists' Paintpots 18

bison 20, 21

Black Dragon's
Cauldron 18

canyons 6

geysers 9, 12-15

gray wolves 21-22

grizzly bears 21-22

hot springs 8-11, 13

Idaho 5

lava 6

magma 9

Mammoth Hot
Springs 11

Montana 5

mountains 6, 24

Mount Washburn 7

mud pots 9, 16-18, 24

Mud Volcano 18

Old Faithful 15

Steamboat Geyser 12, 13

trees 18, 24

volcanoes 6, 9

waterfalls 24

Wyoming 5

Yellowstone River 24

Facts for Now

Visit this Scholastic Web site for more information
on Yellowstone National Park:
www.factsfornow.scholastic.com
Enter the keyword **Yellowstone**

About the Author

Audra Wallace is an editor at Scholastic. She lives with her
family in New York. She enjoys going on adventures to different
places with them.